The Classic Collection

COLLARS TO KNIT AND CROCHET

By The Staff of WORKBASKET Magazine

Kansas City, Missouri

ATTENTION: SCHOOLS AND BUSINESS FIRMS
KC Publishing books are available at quantity discounts for bulk purchases for educational, business or sales promotional use. Call Judy Dawson at (816) 531-5730.

Printed in the United States of America

LIBRARY OF CONGRESS CATALOGING-IN-PUBLICATION DATA

Collars to knit and crochet.
     1. Knitting – Patterns.   2. Crocheting – Patterns.
3. Collars.   I. Workbasket.   II. Series.
TT825.C64 1989   746.9'2   89-3164
ISBN 0-86675-303-6

TABLE OF CONTENTS

PATTERNS

INTRODUCTION

As far back as 1948, The WORK-BASKET published patterns for decorative collars to knit and crochet. These patterns proved very popular with our readers and we have received many requests for reprints.

Because of the renewed interest in and popularity of collars as fashion accessories, The WORK-BASKET staff revised the original published patterns, gathered some new patterns and brought them all together for the first time in this single volume.

In addition to the 26 collar patterns, we included introductory sections from *Aunt Ellen's Knitting Handbook* and *Aunt Ellen's Crochet Handbook*. These sections introduce you to the basic stitches and terminology of each technique, provide general information on the tools and materials you should use to get the best possible results, and offer recommendations for the care of your collars once they are completed.

Though these sections are intended for beginners, experienced knitters and crocheters will find them useful as both a refresher and a handy reference manual.

Each of the 26 collar patterns has been rated: Easy, Intermediate or Experienced. Just remember that all of the designs are simply variations and combinations of the basic stitches.

This book has been carefully organized in logical sequence and you are urged to start at the beginning and read everything carefully. Teach yourself the basics first and then try one of the fabulous collar designs.

CHOOSING THE RIGHT EQUIPMENT AND MATERIALS

Your selection of the right equipment and materials to use in any knit or crochet project will have a great bearing on the beauty and serviceability of your finished work.

First and foremost, use the yarn (or thread) and the size or type of needles (or hook) specified in the instructions to achieve the results the directions promise. It is best to buy extra yarn or thread to assure that you will have enough of the same dye lot to finish the project and to allow for unforeseen usage.

CROCHET HOOKS

A crochet hook is a smooth, slender rod with a dull hook at one end, that is used to catch and draw yarn or thread into interlocking loops. The head of the hook and the shaft of the rod are the same diameter to assure evenness and uniformity of the loops.

Crochet hooks are available in a variety of sizes and are made of metal, plastic or wood. The particular project and your personal preference will determine the crochet hook you select. (A beginner should use only the hook size specified for the project.)

Because the collar patterns included in this book require work with fine thread, all recommend steel hooks. As a general rule, aluminum, plastic and wood are more popular for crocheting with bulky yarn.

KNITTING NEEDLES

It is entirely possible to "knit" just by using your fingers — as in tying knots. Knitting needles simply serve as extensions of your fingers.

Once made of wood, bone and steel, American knitting needles today are made primarily of aluminum, plastic or nylon and their diameters are gauged in ascending order. That is, size 2 is larger than size 1.

All the designs in this book require single-pointed knitting needles, which are available in 10- to 14-inch lengths and sizes 0 to 15.

YARN

Crochet "yarn" is made up of very tightly twisted short fibers. (Even though thread or yarn is used in crochet, reference will be made only to yarn to avoid confusion.) It is generally thin, strong, non-elastic and unyielding. One hundred percent cotton is the most popular, though linens, acrylics and metallics are available.

Knitting yarn is made up of more loosely twisted longer fibers or man-made filaments. It is generally soft, fuzzy, pliable and elastic. Yarn is packaged in skeins, balls or cones and sold by its actual weight. (Length or yardage is often given on the label as well.)

Yarns are dyed in lots or batches and no two lots are precisely the same shade. Thus, manufacturers print the dye lot number on the labels. Be sure to get all you'll need for a project with the same dye lot number.

Where the instructions call for a specific amount of a particular brand of yarn (perhaps not available in your area, thus forcing a substitution) always buy extra with the right to return unbroken packages, because there can be a wide variance in yardage for the same number of ounces (grams) when similar yarn is made by different manufacturers.

UNDERSTANDING THE TERMINOLOGY

Written instructions for both knit and crochet often are confusing to beginners because they appear to be in some kind of mysterious code. Don't be intimidated.

The purpose of this shorthand is three-fold. It speeds up the reading, following and understanding of printed instructions by condensing and shortening them through the use of a few key words or phrases, abbreviations and symbols. Many of these abbreviations are common to both knitting and crocheting and enable you to follow any patterns, no matter the source. They also eliminate boring repetition of instructions.

It is important that you read through all of this special terminology before proceeding to the next section. You can always refer back until you've committed everything to memory through repeated use.

Important terms have been listed alphabetically for easy reference:

BLOCK – Form pieces into proper shape by hand or with the aid of steaming or pressing.
END RIGHT SIDE – Com-

plete a row of the face or outside of the work before going on to the next step.

END WRONG SIDE – Complete a row of the back or inside of the work before going on to the next step.

FASTEN OFF – Cut thread or yarn 4 to 6 inches from work, slip through last loop on hook or needle, pull tight to knot, and weave end into the wrong side of work.

GAUGE – The number of stitches to the inch across a row and the number of rows to the inch vertically.

MARK ROW or STITCH – Loosely tie a contrasting piece of thread, or place a marker or a safety pin at the beginning or end of a row or stitch.

MULTIPLE – Refers to the exact number of stitches needed to complete one pattern design. A multiple of 3 would be any number divisible by 3 (such as 6, 9, 12 and so forth). A multiple of 3 plus 1 would have one more stitch than a multiple of 3 (for example: 7, 10, 13 and so forth).

ROWS – Rows refer to a sequence of stitches in one horizontal line at the end of which the work is turned to begin a new line or row.

TURN – Turn the work around so the reverse side now faces you to begin the next step.

TURNING CHAIN – A quantity of chain stitches made at the end of one row to insure the next row added is the proper height. It often is counted as the first stitch in the next row.

WORK EVEN – Continue working the pattern while neither increasing nor decreasing the row length by adding or omitting any stitches.

At the beginning of any set of pattern instructions to something whose exact size is important (such as a collar), you will find the GAUGE or the number of stitches per inch knitted or crocheted with the specified size needle (or hook) and yarn (or thread).

Because everyone crochets or knits a little differently (some more loosely, some more tightly than others), it is a good idea to make a swatch at least two inches square, block it, then measure it. The number of stitches and rows to the inch should be the same as those given in the instructions. Remember, the size of the needles (or hook) used does not matter as long as your stitch gauge is correct.

Refer back to the special terminology until you've committed everything to memory through repeated use. You'll notice that knitting and crocheting share some common terms.

COMMON ABBREVIATIONS FOR KNIT AND CROCHET

beg	beginning
bl	block
ch	chain
dc	double crochet
dec	decrease
dtr	double treble
hdc	half double crochet
inc	increase
incl	inclusive
k	knit
lp	loop
oz	ounce
p	purl
pat	pattern
pc	picot
psso	pass slip stitch over
rem	remaining
rnd	round
sc	single crochet
sl	slip
sl st	slip stitch
sp	space
st(s)	stitch(es)
tog	together
tr	treble
tr tr	triple treble
yo	yarn over

This symbol * (asterisk) means that the instructions immediately following it are to be repeated the given number of times (in addition to the first) called for in the instructions. For example: *K 4, p 6, repeat from * twice means to knit 4 stitches then purl 6 stitches, then repeat two more times (for a total of 3 times).

Parentheses () indicate that the instructions contained within them are to be repeated. For example: (ch 5, sc in next sc) 5 times means to do everything in the parentheses 5 times in all.

Place markers of some sort on your work at the beginning and end of a set of instructions to be repeated. When the time to repeat comes, you can look back at the work you previously completed and know exactly what you are to repeat. Additional markers will aid in keeping the proper count and in rechecking each step for accuracy before continuing.

To summarize what we've learned in this chapter, printed instructions are a sort of "shorthand recipe" for knitting and crocheting. To be sure that the finished article will be the proper size, you should save yourself a lot of time, trouble and frustration by checking the gauge often.

Now, let's go on to the mechanics of knitting and crocheting.

LEARNING TO KNIT AND CROCHET THE EASY WAY

When it comes to learning to knit or crochet, there is no substitute for practice. Therefore, the sooner you get started, the easier and quicker you will master the skill.

Knitting and crocheting, like tying one's shoes or playing the piano, are two-handed activities for left-handed or right-handed individuals. The important thing is that you learn to knit or crochet in a way that is most comfortable and enjoyable for you.

To eliminate confusion as we get into the actual details, we shall refer to the right hand and the left hand in all instructions and this will apply no matter which hand is favored.

KNITTING

Knitting is a simple technique done for the most part on two needles, but it can fashion garments of delicate beauty or of sturdy warmth and practicality.

In its simplest form, knitting is nothing more than making a series of yarn loops and interlacing them in various ways to form patterns. Thus needles and hands become your knitting machine.

You should concentrate, however, on the yarn and what is happening to it rather than on the position of your hands. The movements of your hands will become easy and routine if you concentrate more on what you are creating than on what you are using to do it.

For practice, take some knitting worsted weight yarn in a bright, pleasing color. Use a pair of number 8 aluminum or plastic knitting needles in a sharply contrasting color so you can study what is happening to the yarn as you work.

Begin by learning the two basic knitting stitches — the KNIT STITCH and the PURL STITCH — which are introduced on the following pages. Only these two are used in knitting. Fancy stitches are a combination of these two stitches as instructed in a particular pattern.

THE SLIPKNOT

The first step in casting on or making any crochet stitch is to form a slipknot. Make a small loop (lp) near the loose end of the yarn or thread by lapping the long strand over the short end. Reach through the loop (lp) and catch the long end of the yarn with the needle or hook and pull it through. Close this slipknot tightly on the shaft of the hook and you've formed your first cast-on stitch or crochet loop (lp).

CASTING ON, ONE-NEEDLE METHOD

To practice, measure off enough yarn for 20 cast-on stitches (we'll call this the tail end) and place a slip knot on the needle as instructed above. Now grasp the needle loosely in the right hand with the tail end of the yarn toward you and the ball end away from you.

Step 1: Loop loose end of the yarn over left thumb and other end of yarn over index finger, bringing both ends of yarn down across palm and holding yarns with remaining fingers.

Step 2: Bring needle under yarn on left thumb.

Step 3: Across and pick up yarn on index finger.

Step 4: Draw yarn through under thumb dropping thumb yarn, tighten (loop stitch) on needle and place thumb in same position as at beginning. Repeat for desired number of stitches.

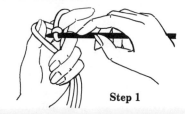

Step 1

Hold needle in right hand with yarn from skein running over index finger. With left hand hold end of yarn in palm with last three fingers. Loop yarn around left thumb.

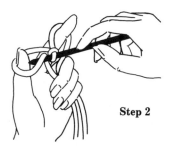

Step 2

Insert needle into loop on thumb from front to back.

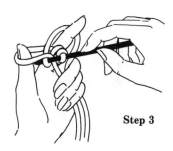

Step 3

Wind yarn in right hand over point of needle from back to front.

Step 4

Pass point of needle through loop on thumb from back to front, easing loop off thumb.

CASTING ON, TWO-NEEDLE METHOD

Place a slipknot on the left needle. Holding needle in left hand, insert right needle through slip knot, pick up yarn with other hand, yarn around right needle, pull yarn through stitch on left needle (one stitch on each needle). Inserting left needle through right stitch from right to left, slip stitch onto left needle and tighten. Continue in this manner for number of stitches desired.

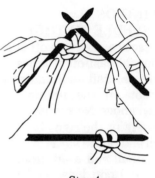

Step 4

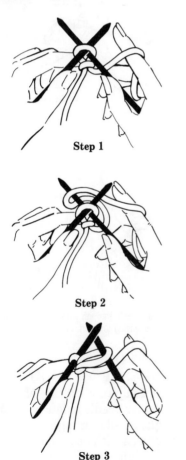

Step 1

Step 2

Step 3

Be sure that all of your stitches (sts) are facing the right way and above all, that they are made loosely enough so you can get your needle and yarn through them easily. Most beginners have a tendency to knit too tightly. Take a moment to study your newly cast-on stitches (sts) so you are conscious of how the yarn loops fit together. Practice casting on until you can do it quickly and easily.

KNIT STITCH (k)

Cast on 20 stitches.

Holding needle with cast-on stitches in left hand, insert right needle into bottom of the first stitch on the left needle, going from the front to back of left needle. Slide the right needle through and upward until the broadest part of the needle rises well above and

ehind the left needle to form a nee-
lle cross.

Holding both needles with left
ingers, pick up yarn in right hand.
Drape around back of index finger,
etting yarn fall across or around
he other fingers to the ball. (The
position of the yarn will be a mat-
er of personal preference. Find out
what works for you.) This draping
around your fingers helps to regu-
ate the yarn tension.

Now, with the yarn in the back,
wrap it counterclockwise around
he right needle. (The yarn is now
between the two needles.) Hold the
yarn snugly and carefully draw
yarn through stitch on left needle,
making a loop on right needle. The
point of the right needle comes
down and back up in front of the
eft needle. Slip worked stitch off
eft needle.

Right needle now holds your first
knit (k) stitch (st). The yarn will be
n back, ready to start the second
st. Repeat the process in each st on
he left needle until it is empty.
Then the right hand needle, holding
all the sts, will be switched to the
eft hand and the process repeated.
By repeating the knit stitch for
several rows, you will have formed
what is called the GARTER
STITCH.

Insert point of empty needle through front of first
cast-on stitch from front to back, passing right
needle under left needle. Always keep yarn BEHIND
work when making knit stitch.

Wrap yarn from skein counterclockwise around
point of right needle.

Draw wrapped yarn through first stitch by bringing
right needle down, under and up in front of left
needle. Right needle holds new loop.

Slide old stitch off left needle – one stitch made.

Take a moment to study what you have done. Are your stitches even, uniformly sized, smooth, all facing the same direction? A common error is to work on the points of the needles rather than being sure that the fat part of the needle is used to "size" each st properly as it is formed.

Note: Never leave your work until you finish a row. Cap the needle point with a point protector to safeguard completed sts.

PURL STITCH (p)

The purl (p) stitch is the only other knitting stitch you need to learn. All other sts are merely combinations of knitting and purling. Therefore, learn to purl well. (It is easy once you realize that purling is the reverse of knitting.)

To start, cast on 20 sts and hold your needles as if you were going to knit (or you can purl onto your last knitted row). Keep the yarn in front of your work at all times when purling, instead of in back as when knitting.

Insert the empty right-hand needle into the lp of the first st from right to left and position the right-hand needle in front of the left-hand needle (again the reverse of knitting). With a counterclockwise motion, wrap the yarn between the two needles and continue around the right needle (yo); complete the stitch as in knitting.

When you've completed a practice row of purling, knit the next row, then purl the next. Alternating rows of knitting with rows of purling is known as the STOCKINETTE STITCH. Practice until you have purling down pat.

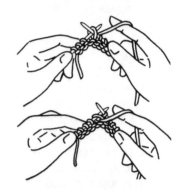

TO SLIP A STITCH (sl)

Insert the right-hand needle into the next stitch as if to purl (unless instructed otherwise), do not yarn over, merely slip the stitch (sl) off the left needle and onto the right needle without either knitting or purling it.

INCREASING (inc)

To increase (inc) in knitting or purling, work one stitch, but do not slip the stitch off the left needle. Instead, work into the back loop of the same stitch (thereby making two stitches out of one), then slip the stitch off the needle.

DECREASING (dec)

To decrease (dec) in knitting or purling, insert the right needle into the loops of the next two stitches, yarn over (thereby making one stitch out of two), slip the stitch off the needle and proceed. Or, slip one stitch, knit or purl one stitch, then pass the slipped stitch over (psso) the knitted or purled stitch.

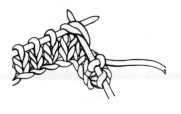

BINDING OFF

To prevent a finished piece from unraveling, instructions will call for binding off a number of stitches. To bind off, knit two stitches onto the right-hand needle in the usual manner.

*Insert the left-hand needle from left to right into the top loop of the first stitch you just knitted across, lift it over the top of the second stitch and let it drop off between the needles (one stitch remains on the right needle). Knit another stitch (again two stitches on right needle). Repeat from * until desired stitches are bound off, then continue knitting as pattern instructs.

FASTEN OFF

Clip the yarn about four inches beyond the last stitch, feed the end through the last stitch on the right-hand needle and pull firmly. When binding off, keep stitches loose to prevent distortion. Always bind off in pattern stitch being worked unless otherwise instructed.

JOINING YARN

When you need to start a new skein of yarn, start a new color or cut out a bad place in the yarn, here are three proven methods of joining. The best way is to drop the end of yarn at the beginning of a row, leaving about a two-inch length, and begin working with the new yarn, leaving a two-inch length. After the article is finished, thread the yarn ends in a blunt needle and weave them in and out for 8 or 10 stitches.

You may also join yarn at the end of a row by making a slipknot with the new strand around the previous strand. Draw slipknot close to end of work.

Another way is to work within 4 inches of end of yarn, then lay a new strand along the old so that about one inch extends beyond last stitch. Knit the four stitches with double yarn, cutting the ends after completion of piece.

CROCHETING

The word crochet is derived from the French word "croché" (crow-SHAY) meaning hook. Originally one of a number of lace-making tools, the hook came to be used alone to fashion a multitude of designs. Because it is so fascinating and versatile, crochet has become a well-loved hand art.

One of the biggest problems beginners have is that they crochet unevenly. Fix in your mind that the diameter size of the crochet hook determines the size of the finished loops (big diameter, big loops; small diameter, small loops). Practice will help adjust yarn tension so the loops (lps) are just right and stay the same size as you progress.

Practice each new stitch over and over again until it becomes easy for you. For each new stitch you learn, make a small practice swatch about four inches square. If you label and keep these practice pieces they can be helpful later as memory joggers for a particular stitch or for project ideas. To begin, grasp the hook in your "working" hand (be that right or left) the way that feels best for you and enables you to work yarn the easiest, but always facing you. Either hold the hook as you would a pencil with the thumb, tips of your index and middle finger (the American way), or hold it like a mixing spoon, with all four fingers wrapped loosely around the shaft and your thumb pressing it against your index finger (the European or Continental way).

Now lay a length of yarn across the palm of your "helping" hand.

With the yarn lying across your palm loose end up, thread it in back of your third finger, under your middle finger and up over your index finger, holding the loose end between your thumb and middle finger. If you need more tension on the yarn, take a turn around your little finger.

First, learn the three basic crochet stitches: the CHAIN STITCH, the SLIP STITCH and the SINGLE CROCHET.

CHAIN STITCH (ch) (st)

Place a slipknot on the shaft of the hook (see slipknot instructions, page 10). With the loop (lp) of the slipknot remaining on the shaft of the hook, wrap the long, ball-end strand of yarn around the hook once. This is known as yarn over (yo). Catch the loop (lp) thus formed with the end of the hook and draw it through the first loop (lp) to form the second stitch (st) in a chain (ch). One loop (lp) always remains on the hook and doesn't count as a stitch (st). Continue in this manner of yarn over (yo), drawing loop (lp) through stitch (st) on hook. This is called a FOUNDATION CHAIN.

As your foundation chain develops, you'll find that grasping it close to where you are working between the thumb and middle finger

of your helping hand will hold the chain still, enabling you to work on it much more easily.

Step 1

Step 2

Now "ch 20 sts." That is, chain 20 stitches, for practice. Be sure to keep an even tension and make all stitches in your chain uniform in size. To be sure your chain is uniform, slide each stitch fully onto the shaft of your hook before beginning the next stitch. Also, be sure your hook is in front of the loose yarn before yarn over to assure your chain being flat, which it must be to work a second row on top. Because the foundation chain is a base upon which all other crochet stitches are made, you will do well to master it before moving to the next step.

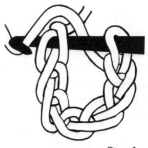

Step 1

SLIP STITCH (sl st)

Whenever you want to join the ends of a chain (ch) to form a ring or round (rnd) or if the instructions say to join, or if an invisible or hidden stitch or row is needed, or if a tight finish is needed along an edge, the slip stitch (sl st) is used.

With the last loop (lp) of a chain (ch) remaining on your hook, go back and insert your hook from the front under the two top strands of the first stitch (st) to be joined, yarn over (yo) and in one motion draw the yarn through both loops (lps) forming a new loop (lp) which remains on the hook. This completes one slip stitch (sl st).

Step 2

SINGLE CROCHET (sc)

One of the most basic and simplest of all crochet stitches is the single crochet (sc) from which all manner of articles can be made. First, make a foundation chain (ch) of 15 stitches. Foundation chains (ch) for single crochet (sc) should always be one more stitch (st) than your single crochet (sc) stitch (st) count, because the odd or last chain st (ch st) is skipped when beginning to single crochet (sc).

Holding the chain (ch) with your helping hand, insert the hook from the front under the two top strands of the second chain (ch) from hook *yarn over (yo) and draw the yarn through the chain (ch) only; there are two loops (lps) on the hook. Next, yarn over (yo) again and draw through both loops (lps); now only one loop (lp) remains on your hook and you've completed your first single crochet (sc). To continue the row, insert your hook in the next chain stitch (st) and repeat from *.

Unless instructed to do otherwise, always insert your hook into the side facing you and always under the two top loops of each stitch.

When the first row is completed (14 sc), chain one stitch (ch 1 st), turn the work so the back or wrong side now faces you, and you are ready to begin your second row.

Whenever TURNING your work, the instructions will specify exactly how many stitches (sts) to chain (ch) because the number varies with the type of stitch (st). The TURNING CHAIN (ch) usually counts as the first stitch (st) in the next row unless otherwise specified. Its main purpose is to bring the piece into proper position for the next row.

After the work has been turned, you'll be working across the row from the opposite or wrong side and it will look different to you. You'll also begin noticing any errors you might have made in the previous row. Should you want to correct such an error, just remove the loop (lp) on your hook, unravel back past the error, put the next available loop (lp) back on your hook and proceed correctly.

*Insert your hook under the two top strands of the first single crochet (sc) stitch, yarn over (yo), draw through this stitch only, to make two loops on your hook. Yarn over (yo) again and pull through both loops to complete the first sc of the second row. Repeat from * in each succeeding stitch (st) in the first row. Continue to work and turn until you have a square. Cut yarn two or three inches after the last stitch, draw the end through the loop on your hook and pull it into a knot to fasten off the work you've done.

Step 1

Note: Had you inserted your hook under the back strand only instead of under the top two strands as you worked your single crochet, you would have gotten a ribbed effect known as a RIB STITCH or SLIPPER STITCH.

INCREASING (inc)

Increasing (inc) in crochet by one stitch is done by working two stitches in one stitch of the previous row or round. The instructions will tell you where to make the increase (inc).

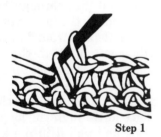

Step 1

Step 2

ROUND (rnd)

In crochet, a round (rnd) refers to work done in one direction with the same side facing all the time. Whether oval, circular, square, oblong or any other shape, it involves increasing wherever the pattern dictates. It is always well to mark the end of each round, so you can check count and accuracy before beginning the next round.

DECREASING (dec)

To learn and practice decreasing (dec) single crochet (sc), work the following.

Row 1: Ch 15, sc in 2nd ch from hook and in each ch across, ch 1, turn.

Row 2: Sc in each st across, ch 1, turn.

Row 3: Decrease (dec) one sc (draw up a loop through each of next 2 stitches, yarn over and draw through 3 loops to make one single crochet), sc in next 10 sc, dec in last 2 sc, ch 1, turn − 12 sc.

Next Row: Follow the pattern in Row 3, working 2 less scs in the middle of each row. Fasten off at the end of any row desired.

Decreasing (dec) in a round (rnd) or the middle of a row is done the same way.

Step 1

JOINING YARN

To start new yarn or a new color, work a stitch up to the last step, pick up the new yarn and complete the last step of the stitch. Keep both loose ends on the wrong side to be woven into the piece later.

BINDING OFF

Patterns with contoured pieces may specify that you bind off four stitches at the beginning of a row. Instead of a turning chain to begin a row, slip stitch across the top of the first five stitches in the row. You've now left four stitches bound off (not worked), and set up the fifth stitch as the base for the next row. Start the next row at this point.

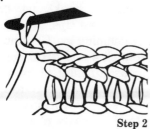

Step 2

MASTERING THE DOUBLES AND TREBLES AND OTHER POPULAR STITCHES

The basic stitches you have learned are the building blocks for the fancy pattern stitches. By using them in various ways and combinations, you can create more intricate designs.

In the basics, you learned to always insert your hook under the top two strands of a stitch, unless otherwise directed. Now, at times you may be asked to insert your hook around or into the bar (or vertical post) of a stitch instead.

Explanations are kept short in order to include all of the more complicated stitches used in the collar patterns. To make working the more complicated patterns easier, have stitch and row markers handy and be sure to keep track of where you are (right side or wrong side, for example).

HALF DOUBLE CROCHET (hdc)

From here on you will notice that each basic stitch you master will be just a little higher and longer than the previous stitch. To make your practice swatch of hdc, ch 16, yo, insert hook into 3rd ch st from hook, yo, draw through ch st only (3 lps on hook), yo, draw through all three lps. You've now completed your first hdc and have only one lp on your hook. Continue to the end of the row, ch 2 and turn. In all rows thereafter the turning ch 2 counts as the first hdc of the new row.

Now yo, skip the first hdc and insert hook into the second hdc, yo, draw through all lps and continue a hdc in each st of the previous row, ch 2, turn, and add as many rows as you wish. Fasten off at the end of any complete row.

In increase (inc), make 2 hdc in any one st. To decrease (dec), yo, insert hook in first st, yo, insert in next st (5 lps on hook), yo, draw through all 5 lps. You've worked off two hdc sts as one st.

DOUBLE CROCHET (dc)

For practice, ch 16, turn, yo, insert hook in 4th ch from hook, yo, draw yarn through ch only (3 lps on hook), yo, draw yarn through two lps only, yo, draw through last two lps. Continue to end of row, ch 3 and turn. For following rows, turning ch of 3 sts counts as first dc in next row, so begin next row of work by inserting hook in second dc of row.

To increase (inc), work 2 dc in one st. To decrease (dec), work one dc to last step in each of next 2 sts, yo, draw through all 3 lps.

TREBLE CROCHET (tr)

Make foundation chain, turn, yo two times, insert hook in 5th ch from hook, yo, draw through 2 lps (now 4 lps on hook), yo, draw through 2 more lps, yo, draw through remaining lps. Continue to end of row, ch 4 and turn. For following rows, turning ch of 4 sts counts as first tr in next row, so begin next row by working in the second tr of previous row.

To increase (inc), work 2 tr in one st. To decrease (dec), work one tr to last step in each of next 2 sts, yo, draw through all 3 lps.

DOUBLE TREBLE CROCHET (dtr)

Make foundation chain, yo hook three times, insert hook in 6th st from hook, work off 2 lps at a time as you did for tr, until st is completed, work double treble crochet (dtr) across row, ch 5, turn.

Next Row: Double treble crochet (dtr) in 2nd st, work as for first row, ch 5, turn. (Each ch 5 counts as dtr).

To increase (inc), work 2 dtr in one st. To decrease (dec), work one dtr to last step in each of next 2 sts, yo, draw through all 3 lps.

TRIPLE TREBLE CROCHET (tr tr)

Make foundation chain, yo hook four times, insert hook in 7th ch from hook, work off 2 lps at a time as you did for treble, continue across row, ch 6, turn.

Next Row: Triple treble (tr tr) in 2nd st, work as for first row, ch 6, turn. (Each ch 6 counts as tr tr).

To increase (inc) work 2 tr tr in one st. To decrease (dec) work one tr tr to last step in each of next 2 sts, yo, draw through all 3 lps.

FILET CROCHET

Filet crochet is made up of open spaces and solid blocks of dc arranged to form designs. To begin a pattern, count the number of spaces and blocks on the first row of a chart or illustration, make a foundation ch allowing 3 chs for each space or block — one extra ch and three more chs to turn if the row begins with a block, 5 more to turn if it begins with a space.

Spaces

Blocks

SOLID SHELL PATTERN

Ch to desired length plus 3 sts.

Row 1: 4 Dc in 4th st from hook, *sk 2 sts, sc in next st, sk 2 sts, 5 dc in next st, repeat from * across, ending row with 1 sc, ch 3, turn.

Row 2: 4 Dc in first sc, *sc in center dc of 5-dc group, 5 dc in next sc, repeat from * across, end with sc in center of last 5 dc group. Repeat Row 2 for pattern. **Note:** Shells may be made with as many dcs as desired.

OPEN SHELL PATTERN

Ch to desired length plus 3 extra sts.

Row 1: Dc in 4th st from hook, (ch 2, 2 dc) in same st, *sk 3 sts, work shell of (2 dc, ch 2, 2 dc) in next st, repeat from * across, ch 3, turn.

Row 2: *Work shell in ch 2 sp of shell in previous row, repeat from * across, making a shell in each ch 2 sp. Repeat Row 2 for pattern.

PICOT (pc)

*Ch 5, sl st back into the first ch at the start of ch 5, sc in each of next 3 sts across, repeat from *.

V-STITCH

Ch to desired length (multiple of 4).

Row 1: Dc in 5th st from hook, ch 3, dc in same st (one V st completed). *Sk 3 sts, dc in next st, ch 3, dc in same st. Repeat from * across to 3rd ch st from end, sk next 2 ch, dc in last ch, ch 3, turn.

Row 2: *Dc in the ch-3 sp of first V st, ch 3, dc in same sp (V over V completed), repeat from * across, dc in top of turning ch, ch 3, turn. Repeat Row 2 for pattern.

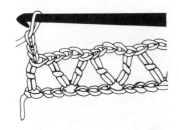

FINISHING

Like the framing of a picture, edges are often added to finished pieces to add body and to keep the edge from rolling or becoming distorted. Slip stitch or single crochet are popular for this purpose. Yarn ends should be threaded into a yarn needle and woven into stitches on wrong side of the work.

WASHING

All of these collars should be hand washed and dried on a smooth, flat surface at room temperature. The top of a clothes dryer provides the quickest results. When washing a hand-made or needle-work garment, be sure to remove any buttons or trims that are not washable.

Press lightly with a steam iron — with spray starch, if desired — through a pressing cloth or man's handkerchief. On raised patterns or plushy natural fiber yarns, just let the steam penetrate well without touching the surface with the iron. Never iron or press synthetic fibers; simply dampen them well, pin garment to original size on toweling with rust-proof pins, and allow to thoroughly dry.

BLOCKING

Blocking is the process of straightening pieces, pressing them flat and truing them up to their proper sizes and dimensions. Lay the collar on heavy paper and trace the outline. After washing, use this outline to reshape garment to original size.

FISHTAIL COLLAR

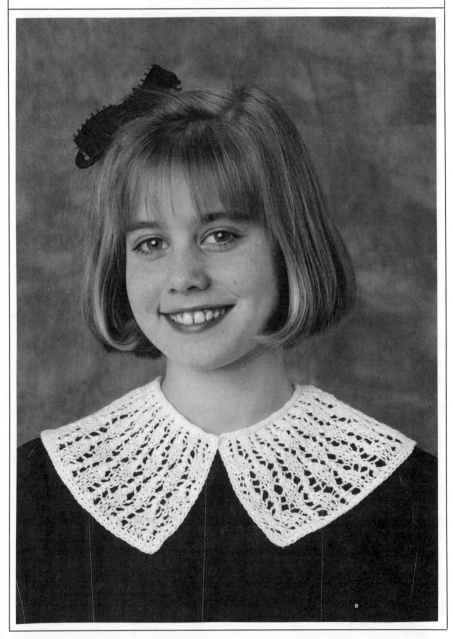

EASY

A knit, spring-weight cotton collar may be worn with a variety of clothing styles from dressy to casual. This versatility makes it a welcome addition to your accessory wardrobe.

You will need 300 yards of Susan Bates "Anchor," numbers 7, 5, 3 and 1 knitting needles, size E crochet hook and a small button.

Note: The Fishtail Pattern Stitch is a multiple of 10 plus 1.

Row 1: K 1, *yo, k 3, sl 1, k 2 tog, psso, k 3, yo, k 1, repeat from * across.

Row 2 and all even rows: Purl.

Row 3: K 1, *k 1, yo, k 2, sl 1, k 2 tog, psso, k 2, yo, k 2, repeat from * across.

Row 5: K 1, *k 2, yo, k 1, sl 1, k 2 tog, psso, k 1, yo, k 3, repeat from * across.

Row 7: K 1, *k 3, yo, sl 1, k 2 tog, psso, yo, k 4, repeat from * across.

Row 8: Purl (p).

Repeat these 8 rows for pattern.

Collar

With number 8 needles, cast on 141 sts and p 1 row. Work 8 rows of the Fishtail Pattern Stitch. Change to number 5 needles and work 8 rows pattern. Change to number 3 needles and work 8 rows pattern. Change to number 1 needles and work 8 rows pattern.

K 1 row.

Decrease as follows: K 5, *sl 1, k 1, psso, k 8, repeat from * to last 4 sts, k 4. K across the next row. Do not fasten off. With crochet hook and right side facing, work 1 row sc around collar, working 3 scs in corners. Before last st on right front edge, ch 4; work last sc in last st. This makes a lp for button. Sew button opposite the lp or use a decorative pin at neck edge.

ECRU COLLAR

Knit and purl stitches combine to create a rosary pattern for this attractive collar, shown here in ecru or ivory. Quick and easy to make, it would be a lovely gift for a young girl's graduation or a fast-selling entry in your club's next bazaar.

You will need one ball of crochet cotton, numbers 8, 7, 5, 3 and 1 knitting needles, a size E crochet hook and a small button.

Rosary Pattern Stitch

Rows 1 and 3: K 2, *yo, k 2, sl 1, k 2 tog, psso, k 2, yo, K 1*, k 1.

Rows 2, 4, 6, 8: P the yo's and sts.

Rows 5 and 7: K 1, k 2 tog, *k 2, yo, k 1, yo, k 2, sl 1, k 2 tog, psso*, end with sl 1, k 1, psso, k 1.

Collar

Repeat these 8 rows for pattern.

With number 8 needles, cast on 131 sts. Change to number 7 needles and p 1 row. Work 8 pattern rows. Change to number 5 needles, work 8 pattern rows. Change to number 3 needles, work 8 pattern rows. Change to number 1 needles, work 8 pattern rows. K 1 row on k side of work, k next row on p side of work. Bind off. Work 1 row sc around collar working 3 sc's each point. Crochet small lp on right side of collar for button. (If desired, snap closing or dressy pin may be used.) Work in ends, block.

PETER PAN COLLAR

T his whimsical creation would be the perfect gift for that special teenage niece on her next birthday. Two different yarns, worked together, create an unusual color and texture.

One size fits all. Neck measures 14 inches around. Depth from neck to outside edge is 5 inches.

Use 1 skein (56 grams) Coats & Clark's "Lustersheen" in natural, 1 skein (50 grams) Berroco "Dante" in ecru, a size G crochet hook and number 11 knitting needles or size required for given gauge.

Gauge: 3 sts equal 1 inch in garter st (k every row) using two strands of yarn held tog and

EASY

worked as one.
TO SAVE TIME, TAKE TIME TO CHECK GAUGE.
Starting at neck edge, cast on 43 sts. K 4 rows for border. Work pattern as follows:

Row 1: (Right Side) K 3, yo, sl 1, k 2 tog, psso, yo, k 3; (yo, k 1, yo, k 3) two times; (yo, sl 1, k 2 tog, psso, yo, k 3) two times; (yo, k 1, yo, k 3) two times; yo, sl 1, k 2 tog, psso, yo, k 3 — 51 sts.

Row 2 and all even rows: K 3 for border, p across to last 3 sts, k 3.

Row 3: K 6, *yo, sl 1, k 2 tog, psso; (yo, k 1) three times; repeat from * one time; (yo, sl 1, k 2 tog, psso, yo, k 3) two times. **Yo, sl 1, k 2 tog, psso, (yo, k 1) three times; repeat from ** one time, ending yo, sl 1, k 2 tog, psso, yo, k 6 — 59 sts.

Row 5: K 3, yo, sl 1, k 2 tog, psso, yo; (k 3, yo, k 1, yo) four times; (k 3, yo, sl 1, k 2 tog, psso, yo) two times; (k 3, yo, k 1, yo) four times; k 3, yo, sl 1, k 2 tog, psso, yo, k 3 — 75 sts.

Row 7: K 6, yo, sl 1, k 2 tog, psso, yo; *k 3, yo, sl 1, k 2 tog, psso, yo, repeat from * around ending k 6 — 75 sts.

Row 9: (K 3, yo, sl 1, k 2 tog, psso, yo) two times; (k 1, yo) three times; sl 1, k 2 tog, psso, yo, k 3, yo, sl 1, k 2 tog, psso, yo; (k 1, yo) three times; sl 1, k 2 tog, psso, yo; (k 3, yo, sl 1, k 2 tog, psso, yo) three times; (k 1, yo) three times; sl 1, k 2 tog, psso, yo, k 3, yo, sl 1, k 2 tog, psso; (yo, k 1) three times; (yo, sl 1, k 2 tog, psso, yo, k 3) two times — 83 sts.

Row 11: K 6, *yo, sl 1, k 2 tog, psso, yo, k 3; (yo, k 1, yo, k 3) two times; repeat from * across one time; (yo, sl 1, k 2 tog, psso, yo, k 3) three times; (yo, k 1, yo, k 3) two times; yo, sl 1, k 2 tog, psso, yo, k 3; (yo, k 1, yo, k 3) two times; yo, sl 1, k 2 tog, psso, yo, k 6 — 99 sts.

Row 13: K 3, *yo, sl 1, k 2 tog, psso, yo, k 3, repeat from * around — 99 sts.

Row 14: Repeat Row 2.

Rows 15-19: K.

Bind off loosely.

Button Loops: With right side facing, size G crochet hook and 2 strands of yarn held tog, make 3 lps on right collar edge. At bottom edge, join with a sl st, ch 5, sk a finger's width, join with a sl st and fasten off. Repeat for lp for other two lps. Weave in loose ends.

Yarn Buttons: Make small balls of yarn that will fit into the button lp. Fasten off leaving about 8 inches. Sew into button to secure yarn. Sew button to collar.

OPEN WORK RIB KNIT COLLAR

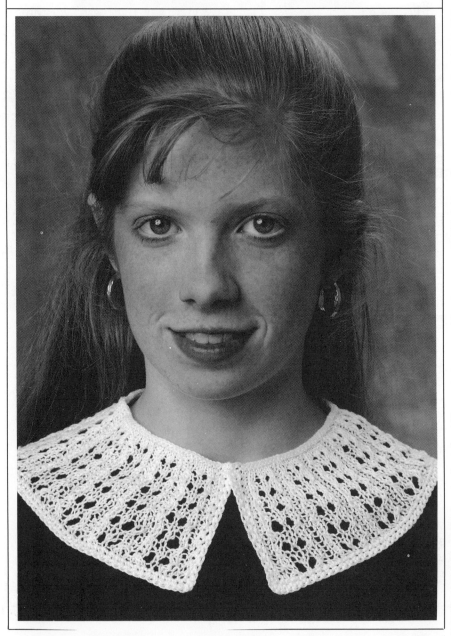

EASY

Alternating knit and purl rows create the classic "ribbed" or "fish tail" effect for this collar. The loose, traditional styling make it appropriate for any age, any season, any occasion.

You will need one ball of white crochet cotton, numbers 8, 7, 5, 3 and 1 knitting needles and size E crochet hook.

Ribbed Pattern

Row 1: K 1, *p 2, k 2 tog, yo, k 1, yo, sl 1, k 1, psso*, repeat between *'s to last 3 sts, p 2, k 1.

Rows 2 and 4: P 1, k 2, *p 5, k 2*, repeat between *'s, end with p 1.

Row 3: K 1, *p 2, k 5, repeat between *'s to last 3 sts, p 2, k 1.

Repeat these four rows for pattern.

Collar

With number 8 needles, cast on 137 sts, p 1 row. Change to number 7 needles and work 8 rows of pattern. Change to number 5 needles and work 8 rows of pattern. Change to number 3 needles and work 4 rows of pattern. Change to number 1 needles and work 4 rows of pattern. Do not fasten off.

K next 2 rows (the 2nd row will be the p side). Bind off sts. With crochet hook and right side facing, start at left neck edge and work sc around collar, working 3 sc's in each corner. (Do NOT crochet around neck edge.) Turn and work sc in each st around collar. Fasten off and work in ends. Steam press lightly.

KNIT ANGORA COLLAR

This soft and pretty collar with a zigzag pattern is well suited to any age. It would sell well at your next church or club bazaar.

You will need one 20 gram ball Bernat's "Dreamspun," a blend of 70% angora and 30% lambswool. You will also need one pair each numbers 1, 3 and 5 standard knitting needles (or size required to obtain given gauge), a size F crochet hook and one small button.

Directions are given for a 13½-inch neck measurement, with changes for a 14½-inch neck given in parentheses.

Pattern Rows: Multiple of 13 plus 2

Row 1: P 2, *yo, k 4, sl 1, k 2 tog, psso, k 4, yo, p 2, repeat from * across.

Row 2 and all even rows: K 2, p 11, k 2, repeat from * across.

Row 3: P 2, *k 1, yo, k 3, sl 1, k 2 tog, psso, k 3, yo, k 1, p 2, repeat from * across.

Row 5: P 2, *k 2, yo, k 2, sl 1, k 2 tog, psso, k 2, yo, k 2, p 2, repeat from * across.

Row 7: P 2, *k 3, yo, k 1, sl 1, k 2 tog, psso, k 1, yo, k 3, p 2, repeat from * across.

Row 9: P 2, *k 4, yo, sl 1, k 2 tog, psso, yo, k 4, p 2, repeat from * across.

Row 10: Repeat Row 2.

Repeat Rows 1 through 10 for pattern.

With larger needles, cast on 132 (145). P 1 row. Repeat Pattern Rows 1 through 10.

Change to medium-sized needles and work pattern rows once.

Change to small needles and work pattern rows once.

K 1 row, p 1 row, k 2 rows, bind off.

With right side facing, join yarn with crochet hook at left neck edge. Sc in each st around, working 3 sc in each point. On each front edge, sc will be in every other st. Before working into last st on right front edge, ch 4, work sc in last st (button lp made). Work in ends and block. Sew button opposite loop.

TULIP PATTERNED COLLAR

By using a variety of sizes of knitting needles and alternating rows of knitting and purling stitches, you will create this tasteful, contemporary tulip-patterned collar. Give it to the flower enthusiast in your family for her birthday. You will need one skein of Red Heart "Luster Sheen," size E crochet hook and knitting needles numbers 9, 7, 5, 3 and 1.

Pattern Rows

Row 1: P.

Row 2: K.

Row 3: K 1, p 6, *(p 1, k 1, p 1, k 1, p 1, k 1) in next st, p 12, repeat from * across, ending with (p 1, k 1, p 1, k 1, p 1, k 1), p 6, k 1.

Row 4: K 7, *p 6, k 12, repeat from * across, ending with p 6, k 7.

Row 5: K 1, p 6, *k 6, p 12, repeat from * across, ending with k 6, p 6, k 1.

Row 6: Repeat Row 4.

Row 7: K 1, p 2 tog twice, p 2, *k 2, yo, k 2, yo, k 2, p 2, p 2 tog 4 times, p 2, repeat from * across, ending with k 2, yo, k 2, yo, k 2, p 2, p 2 tog twice, k 1.

Row 8: K 5, *p 8, k 8, repeat from * across, ending with p 8, k 5.

Row 9: K 1, p 2 tog twice, *k 2 tog, yo, k 1, yo, k 2 tog, yo, k 1, yo, k 2 tog, p 2 tog 4 times, repeat from * across, ending with p 2 tog twice, k 1.

Row 10: K 3, *p 9, k 4, repeat from * across, ending with p 9, k 3.

Collar

Using number 9 needles, cast on 132 sts. P one row. Change to number 7 needles and work 10 pattern rows. Change to number 5 needles and work 10 pattern rows. Change to number 3 needles and work 10 pattern rows. Change to number 1 needles and p 1 row, k 1 row and p 2 rows. Bind off. Do not fasten off. Work one row sc around collar, but not around neck edge. Turn and work 1 row sc in each sc around. Work 3 sc in corners.

Weave in ends.

BEAR PAW COLLAR

INTERMEDIATE

I f you look closely at the lacy pattern of this collar and use your imagination, you will see a bear's paw in the design. This unusual pattern is made by alternating rows of knitting and purling. You will need one ball Susan Bates "Fashion Tone" number 8 mercerized cotton (300 yards per ball), Susan Bates knitting needles numbers 9, 7, 5, 3 and 1 and a size D crochet hook.

Pattern Stitch

Row 1: *K 2, (p 4, k 1) 3 times, p 4, k 2, repeat from * across.

Row 2 and all even rows: P the p sts, k the yo's and k sts.

Row 3: *K 1, yo, k 1, p 2, p 2 tog, (k 1, p 4) twice, k 1, p 2 tog, p 2, k 1, yo, k 1, repeat from * across.

Row 5: K 2, yo, k 1, p 3, k 1, p 2, p 2 tog, k 1, p 2 tog, p 2, k 1, p 3, k 1, yo, k 2, repeat from * across.

Row 7: *K 3, yo, k 1, p 1, p 2 tog, (k 1, p 3) twice, k 1, p 2 tog, p 1, k 1, yo, k 3, repeat from * across.

Row 9: *K 4, yo, k 1, p 2, k 1, p 1, p 2 tog, k 1, p 2 tog, p 1, k 1, p 2, k 1, yo, k 4, repeat from * across.

Row 11: *K 5, yo, k 1, p 2 tog, (k 1, p 2) twice, k 1, p 2 tog, k 1, yo, k 5, repeat from * across.

Row 13: *K 6, yo, k 1, p 1, k 1, (p 2 tog, k 1) twice, p 1, k 1, yo, k 6, repeat from * across.

Row 14: Repeat Row 2.

Collar

Using number 9 needles, cast on 138 sts. Change to number 7 needles and work Rows 1-10 of pattern. Change to number 5 needles and work pattern Rows 11-14, then work pattern Rows 1-4. Change to number 3 needles and work pattern Rows 5-10. Change to number 1 needles and work pattern Rows 11-14. K 2 rows. Bind off.

With wrong side facing and size D hook, join yarn and work 2 rnds sc, working 3 sc in each corner. **Note:** On neck edge, work scs in front lp of bound off sts.

Weave in ends and block.

SNOWDROP COLLAR

Knitting and purling stitches alternate to produce this lacy collar that is as delicate in detail as a snowflake. It might look difficult to make, but it isn't.

You will need one ball of Pearl Twist crochet cotton, size E crochet hook and numbers 9, 7, 5, 3 and 1 knitting needles.

Pattern Stitch

Rows 1 and 3: K 1, *yo, dbl dec (k 2 tog through back loop, place this st on left needle and pass the st next to this st over the st you placed on the needle, then replace this st back on the right needle), yo, k 5, repeat from * across, ending with yo, dbl dec, yo, k 1.

Rows 2, 4, 6 and 8: Purl.

Row 5: K 1, *k 3, yo, sl 1, k 1, psso, k 1, k 2 tog, yo, k 3, repeat from * across, ending with k 4.

Row 7: K 1, *yo, dbl dec, yo, k 1, repeat from * across, ending with yo, dbl dec, yo, k 1.

Collar

Using number 9 needles, cast on 133 sts and p 1 row.

Change to number 7 needles and work 8 rows of pattern. Work 8 rows of pattern using number 5 needles and then work 8 rows of pattern using number 3 needles. Change to number 1 needles and work rows 1 and 2 of pattern, continuing as follows:

Row 3: K 1, *yo, dbl dec, yo, k 1, repeat from * across.

Row 4: Purl.

Row 5 and 6: Knit.

Bind off. Do **NOT** fasten off yarn. Using crochet hook, crochet 1 row sc around collar, working 3 sts in corners. Turn and work reverse sc around collar. Fasten off. Work in ends and block.

OPEN WORK COLLAR

EASY

C omposed primarily of the knit stitch and yarn over, this collar is an excellent project for the beginning knitter.

Using number 4 needles, cast on 20 sts.

Rows 1, 2, 3: K.

Row 4: K 6, (yo, k 2 tog) 6 times, k 1, yo, k 1 — 21 sts. Cast on 6 sts at end of this row — 27 sts.

Rows 5, 7, 9 and 11: K.

Row 6: K 7, k 2 tog, (k 1, k 2 tog) 5 times, k 2, yo, k 1 — 22 sts.

Row 8: K 19, yo twice, k 2 tog, yo, k 1 — 24 sts.

Note: On return Rows 9, 11 and 13, be sure to work a k st in both lps of yo twice.

Row 10: K 6, (yo twice, k 2 tog) 6 times, k 5, yo, k 1 — 31 sts.

Row 12: K 7, k 2 tog, (k 1, k 2 tog) 5 times, k 3, yo twice, k 2 tog, yo, k 2 — 27 sts.

Row 13: K 21, turn (this shapes neck).

Row 14: Sl last k st in Row 13 to right needle, k remaining 20 sts.

Row 15: Bind off 7 sts loosely, p 20.

Repeat pattern Rows 4-15 for desired length.

Edging: With size F hook, sc along side of collar, 3 sc in corner st, sc along edge of point, 6 dc in center of point, continue around each point and down other side. Fasten off.

SUNBURST COLLAR

Don't be surprised if you receive many compliments from your friends and relatives when you greet them wearing this delicate crocheted collar. Just smile and say, "Thanks. I made it myself."

You will need two balls of Coats

& Clark's "Knit-Cro-Sheen," a size 10 steel crochet hook and a hook-and-eye fastener.

To begin, make a ch about 16 inches long.

Row 1: Dc in 4th ch from hook, dc in each of next 2 ch, *(ch 5, sk 3 ch, sc in next ch) 3 times, ch 5, sk 3 ch, dc in each of next 4 ch, repeat from * until there are 8 ch lp sections. The row should measure about 15 inches. Ch 3, turn.

Row 2: Sk first dc, dc in each of next 3 dc, *ch 3, sc in next lp, (ch 5, sc in next lp) 3 times, ch 3, dc in each of next 4 dc, repeat from * across, making last dc in top of turning ch, ch 3, turn.

Row 3: Sk first dc, dc in each of next 3 dc, *ch 3, sc in next lp, (ch 5, sc in next lp) 4 times, ch 3, dc in each of next 4 dc, repeat from * across, making last dc in top of turning ch, ch 3, turn.

Row 4: Sk first dc, dc in each of next 3 dc, *ch 5, sk ch-3 lp, sc in next ch-5 lp, (ch 5, sc in next ch-5 lp) 3 times, ch 5, sk ch-3 lp, dc in each of next 4 dc, repeat from * across, making last dc in top of turning ch, ch 3, turn.

Row 5: Repeat Row 3, having 4 ch-5 lps between ch-3 lps, ch 3, turn.

Row 6: Sk first dc, dc in each of next 3 dc, *ch 3, sc in next ch-3 lp, (ch 5, sc in next lp) 5 times, ch 3, dc in each of next 4 dc, repeat from * across, making last dc in top of turning ch, ch 3, turn.

Row 7: Sk first dc, dc in each of next 3 dc, *ch 5, sk ch-3 lp, sc in next ch-5 lp, (ch 5, sc in next ch-5 lp) 4 times, ch 5, dc in each of next 4 dc, repeat from * across, ch 3, turn.

Row 8: Repeat Row 2, having 5 ch-5 lps between ch-3 lps.

Row 9: Repeat Row 7.

Row 10: Repeat Row 8.

Row 11: Repeat Row 2, having 6 ch-5 lps between ch-3 lps.

Row 12: Repeat Row 2, having 7 ch-5 lps between ch-3 lps.

Row 13: Sk first dc, dc in each of next 3 dc, *ch 5, sk ch-3 lp, sc in next ch-5 lp, (ch 5, sc in next ch-5 lp) 6 times, ch 5, dc in each of next 4 dc, repeat from * across, ch 1, turn.

Row 14: Sc in each of next 4 dc, *5 sc in each of next 8 lps, sc in each of next 4 dc, repeat from * across. Fasten off.

Neckband: Join thread at base of first dc.

Row 1: Ch 1, sc in each ch across, ch 5, turn.

Row 2: Sk 2 sc, dc in next sc, *ch 2, sk 2 sc, dc in next sc, repeat from * across. Fasten off.

Lightly press and starch. Sew on hook-and-eye closure.

SHELL STITCH LACE COLLAR

I magine this pretty collar complementing your favorite sweater. It can be easily, quickly and inexpensively made by following these simple instructions.

To make it, you need one ball of size 30 mercerized cotton thread and a size 3 steel crochet hook.

Gauge: 8 dc equal 1 inch

Row 1: Ch 126, dc in 4th ch from hook, dc in each of the next 123 ch across, ch 3, turn.

Row 2: 3 Dc in first dc (shell made), ch 4, *sk 4 dc, 3 dc in next dc. Repeat from * across, ending row with 1 dc, ch 3, turn – 25 shells made.

Row 3: *4 Dc in peak of each 3-dc shell, ch 4, repeat from * across, ending row with 1 dc, ch 3, turn.

Row 4: *5 Dc in peak of 4-dc shell, ch 2, 1 dc around ch in Rows 2 and 3, ch 2, repeat from * across, ending row with 1 dc, ch 3, turn.

Row 5: *6 Dc in peak of 5-dc shell, ch 4, repeat from * across, ending row with 1 dc, ch 3, turn.

Row 6: *7 Dc in peak of 6-dc shell, ch 4, repeat from * across, ending row with 1 dc, ch 3, turn.

Row 7: *8 Dc in peak of 7-dc shell, ch 2, 1 dc around chs in rows 5 and 6, ch 2, repeat from * across, ending with 1 dc.

Fasten off.

JABOT COLLAR

T his unique collar with jabot offers the possibility of two accessories in one. For a subtle touch of lace, wear the col- lar alone. Or, snap the jabot over the collar's hook-and-eye for a dressier look.

Whichever you prefer, the various

pieces are easy to make and will be a welcome addition to your accessory collection.

To make both the jabot and the collar, you will need 210 yards size 5 DMC Pearl Cotton, size 1 steel crochet hook (or size required to obtain given gauge), one snap and a hook-and-eye fastener.

Gauge: 7 sc equal 1 inch

TO SAVE TIME, TAKE TIME TO CHECK GAUGE.

COLLAR

Ch 110 to measure approximately 15 inches.

Row 1: Sc in 2nd ch from hook and in each ch across — 109 sc. Ch 3, turn.

Row 2: 2 Dc in first sc, ch 2, 2 dc in same sc, *sk 2 sc, (2 dc, ch 2, 2 dc) shell in next sc, repeat from * across — 37 shells. Ch 3, turn.

Row 3: (2 Dc in first ch-2 sp, ch 2, 2 dc) shell in same sp, work shell in each ch-2 sp across, end dc in top of ch-3. Ch 3, turn.

Repeat Row 3 five more times. Do not fasten off. Ch 4, turn.

Edging: 5 Tr in first ch-2 sp, *sc in next ch-2 sp, 10 tr in next ch-2 sp, repeat from * across, ending last repeat with 6 tr in last ch-2 sp. Do not fasten off.

Work 1 row sc up collar front, around neck edge, then down other side of front, fasten off. Sew hook-and-eye to collar edge.

JABOT

Make two separate pieces — 1 long and 1 short.

Long Piece: Ch 26, sc in 2nd ch from hook and in each ch across — 25 sc. Ch 3, turn.

Row 1: Repeat Row 2 of collar — 9 shells.

Row 2: Repeat Row 3 of collar until 13 rows have been worked, do not fasten off. Ch 4, turn.

Edging: 5 tr in first ch-2 sp, *sc in next ch-2 sp, 10 tr in next ch-2 sp, repeat from * across, ending last repeat with 6 tr in last ch-2 sp. Fasten off.

Short Piece: Work as for long piece until 10 rows have been completed, do not fasten off. Repeat edging as for long piece.

Tabs: Row 1: Working through top edges of both long and short pieces at the same time, join yarn and work double dec across as follows: pull up lp in each of next 3 sts, yo and pull through all sts on hook.

Rows 2 through 10: Work even in sc, fasten off at end of Row 10.

Finishing: Sew snap to lower edge of tab and to back of jabot. Snap around collar at neck opening.

COBWEB
RIB KNIT COLLAR

EASY

I t is easy to see why this thicker, wintry collar is called "the cobweb." Besides being beautiful and versatile, it is easy, quick and inexpensive to make. All you need is one ball of white sport yarn, a size G aluminum crochet hook, and one ¼-inch pearlized shank button. Directions are given to fit an 18-inch neck.

To begin, ch 61.

Row 1: Sc in 2nd and 3rd chs from hook, ch 1, *sc in each of next 2 ch, ch 1, repeat from * across, sc in each of last 2 ch, ch 1, turn.

Row 2: Sc in first st, ch 2, *sc in ch-1 sp, ch 2, repeat from * across, sc in last sc, ch 1, turn.

Row 3: Sc in first st, 2 sc in ch-2 lp, *ch 1, 2 sc in ch-2 lp, repeat from * across, sc in last sc, ch 1, turn.

Row 4: Sc in first st, ch 3, *sc in ch-1 sp, ch 3, repeat from * across, sc in last sc, ch 1, turn.

Row 5: Sc in first st, 3 sc in ch-3 lp, *ch 1, 3 sc in ch-3 lp, repeat from * across, sc in last sc, ch 1, turn.

Row 6: Sc in first st, ch 4, *sc in ch-1 sp, ch 4, repeat from * across, sc in last sc, ch 1, turn.

Row 7: Sc in first st, 4 sc in ch-4 lp, *ch 1, 4 sc in ch-4 lp, repeat from * across, sc in last sc, ch 1, turn.

Row 8: Sc in first st, ch 5, *sc in ch-1 sp, ch 5, repeat from * across, sc in last sc, ch 1, turn.

Row 9: Sc in first st, 5 sc in ch-5 lp, *ch 1, 5 sc in ch-5 lp, repeat from * across, sc in last sc, ch 1, turn.

Row 10: Sc in first st, ch 6, *sc in ch-1 sp, ch 6, repeat from * across, sc in last sc, ch 1, turn.

Row 11: Sc in first st, 6 sc in ch-6 lp, *ch 1, 6 sc in ch-6 lp, repeat from * across, sc in last sc, ch 1, turn.

Row 12: Sc in first st, ch 7, *sc in ch-1 sp, ch 7, repeat from * across, sc in last sc, ch 1, turn.

Row 13: Sc in first st, 7 sc in ch-7 lp, *ch 1, 7 sc in ch-7 lp, repeat from * across, sc in last sc, ch 1. Do not turn.

Edging: Sc in same sp as last sc, 1 sc in end of each row along edge of collar, 3 sc in corner, 1 sc in each ch along neck edge, 3 sc in corner, 1 sc in end of each row along edge of collar, 3 sc in corner, 1 sc in each of next 4 sc, ch 3, sl st in first ch (picot made), *sc in each of next 4 sc, picot, repeat from * across, ending with 1 sc in each of last 3 sc, 2 sc in corner st. Join with sl st, fasten off. Sew button to back of collar.

TIED COLLAR

T his collar, which ties in the front, is easy to make because it is crocheted with the simplest of stitches. Its contemporary style is an appropriate accent for silk or denim.

You will need 1 ball (400 yards) of Bucilla "Wondersheen" and size 6 steel crochet hook, or size required to obtain gauge.

EASY

Gauge: 4 spaces equal 1 inch;
11 rows equal 3 inches
TO SAVE TIME, TAKE TIME TO CHECK GAUGE.

Ch 108.

Row 1: Sc in 2nd ch from hook and in each ch across — 107 sc. Ch 4, turn.

Row 2: Sk 1 sc, dc in next sc, *sk 1 sc, ch 1, dc in next sc, repeat from * across — 53 filet spaces. **Note:** Last dc is always worked in 3rd st of turning ch of last row. Ch 4, turn.

Row 3: Sk sp, dc in next dc, *sk sp, ch 1, dc in next dc, repeat from * across. Ch 4, turn. Repeat Row 3 for 6 inches or until desired length.

Neck Shaping and Left Side:

Row 1: Work across 14 filet sps, do not ch 1, dc in next dc. Ch 3, turn.

Row 2: Sk sp, ch 3, dc in next dc, *ch 1, sk sp, dc in next dc, repeat from * across — 13 sps. Ch 4, turn.

Work even over 13 filet spaces for 5 more rows. Ch 4, turn.

Row 8: Dc in first dc (counts as turning ch) — 1 filet increased. Finish row in established pattern. Ch 4, turn.

Row 9: Work across in established pattern. Ch 4, turn.

Repeat Rows 8 and 9 once, repeat Row 8 once more — 16 filet spaces.

Row 13: Work across 16 filet spaces, ch 23 for front of neckline.

Row 14: Dc in 6th ch from hook, *ch 1, sk 1 ch, dc in next ch, repeat from * 10 times, continue working in established pattern across row — 26 filet spaces. Ch 4, turn.

Row 15: Sk sp, dc in next dc, work across in established pattern. Ch 4, turn.

Rows 16-19: Work in established pattern across 26 filet spaces.

Row 20: Work in established pattern across, do not work in turning ch — 25 filet spaces. Ch 3, turn. Continue in established pattern, dec one st at outside edge every 2 rows until one space remains. Fasten off.

Neck Shaping and Right Side:

Skip 25 dc for neck, join thread in 26th dc.

Row 1: Ch 3, dc in next dc, *ch 1, sk 1 sp, dc in next dc, repeat from * across. Ch 4, turn — 14 filet spaces. Continue working right side of collar, reversing shapings until 1 sp remains. Fasten off.

Finishing: With right side facing, join thread to back of collar at right edge.

Row 1: Work 1 row sc around collar, working approximately 2 sc in each filet sp, ending at back on left edge. **Note:** There is already 1 row sc across back of collar.

Row 2: *Ch 3, sk 2 sc, sc in next sc, continue around collar. Fasten off. Sew hook-and-eye invisibly at neck edge.

METALLIC CORDÉ COLLAR

This distinctive metallic cordé collar may be made with a combination of angora or textured yarns. Choose yarn in a basic color such as gold, silver, white or blue. The collar measures about three inches wide at the points. Pearls, teardrops or buttons may be sewn to the points, if desired.

The original model was made of gold metallic cordé (about 60 yards). This model is made in blue Knit-Cro-Sheen. You will also need size 4 or 5 steel crochet hook.

Ch 97.

Row 1: Sc in second st from hook, sc in each st across row, ch 3, turn.

Row 2: Dc in next sc, *sk 1 st, dc in next st, ch 3, dc in same st as the previous dc, sk next st, dc in each of next 2 sc, repeat from * across row, ch 3, turn.

Row 3: Work this row rather loosely. Dc in next dc, *sk 1 dc, dc over ch 3 of previous row, ch 3, dc in same place, sk next dc, dc in each of next 2 dcs, repeat from * across row, ch 3, turn.

Row 4: Same as previous row, only add a ch st between the dc's on each side of the ch-3, ch 3, turn.

Row 5: Repeat Row 4, crocheting loosely.

Row 6: Same as previous row, only make a ch-4 instead of ch-3.

Row 7: Ch 1, sc in each st across. For a smooth and flat finish work in one loop only of each stitch. Fasten off.

Fasten the collar together with a hook-and-eye closure or with ties as shown. To make the ties, make 2 chains, each 12 to 14 inches long. Sc in each ch st for a flat, firm tie.

For round ties, make 2 chains 12 to 14 inches long, sl st in each ch. End leaving enough thread to sew to collar.

BLACK COLLAR

dd this elegant, scalloped accent to any holiday sweater or dress. Black is an attractive color no matter what the occasion, day or night.

You will need 1 skein (400 yards) "Wondersheen" in black, size 6 steel crochet hook (or size to obtain given gauge) and 1 black button.

Gauge: 3 shells equal 1 inch
TO SAVE TIME, TAKE TIME TO CHECK GAUGE.

To begin, ch 142.

Row 1: Dc in 5th ch from hook, ch 1, dc in same ch, *sk 1 ch, (dc, ch 1, dc) shell in next ch, repeat from * across to last 2 ch, sk 1 ch, dc in last ch. Ch 2, turn.

Row 2: *(Dc, ch 1, dc) shell in next sp, repeat from * across, end dc in top of turning ch. Ch 2, turn.

Row 3: Repeat Row 2.

Row 4: *(Dc, ch 1, dc) shell in next sp, (dc, ch 2, dc) shell in next sp, repeat from * across, dc in top of turning ch. Ch 2, turn.

Row 5: Repeat Row 4.

Row 6: *(Dc, ch 2, dc) shell in next sp, repeat from * across, dc in top of turning ch. Ch 2, turn.

Row 7: Repeat Row 6.

Row 8: Ch 5, sc in first sp, *ch 5, sc in next sp, ch 5, sk 1 sp, sc in next sp, repeat from * across, end last repeat ch 2, dc in turning ch. Ch 1, turn.

Row 9: Sc in dc, ch 5, *sc in sc, ch 3, (2 dc, ch 1, 2 dc) shell in ch-5 sp, ch 3, sc in sc, ch 5, sc in ch-5 sp, ch 5, repeat from * across, end last repeat sc in sc, ch 3, (2 dc, ch 1, 2 dc) shell in ch-5 sp, ch 3, sc in sc, ch 2, dc in turning ch. Turn.

Row 10: *Ch 5, sc in top of ch-3, ch 3, (2 dc, ch 1, 2 dc) shell in ch-1 sp, ch 3, sc in top of ch-3, (ch 5, sc in next ch-5 sp) twice, repeat from * across, end last repeat (ch-5, sc in ch-5 sp) once. Turn.

Row 11: *Ch 5, sc in ch-5 sp, ch 5, sc in top of ch-3, ch 3, (2 dc, ch 1, 2 dc) shell in ch-1 sp, ch 3, sc in top of ch-3, (ch 5, sc in next ch-5 sp) twice, repeat from * across, end last repeat ch 5, sc in ch-5 sp. Turn.

Row 12: Repeat Row 11, working 1 more (ch 5, sc in ch-5 sp) between shells. Do not fasten off at end of row. Work 1 row sc along front edge of collar, fasten off.

Join thread at opposing front neck edge. From wrong side, work 1 sc along neck edge holding in to about 19 inches or desired size. Ch 6 sts for button lp, turn and work one more row sc along neck edge. Work 2 sc in end st and continue down front edge, fasten off. Sew button opposite lp.

CLASSIC COLLAR

This pattern for a crocheted collar will enable you to make both a family heirloom and a modern, individual fashion statement. The collar is designed for a jewel neckline.

Materials needed are a 450 yard ball of number 20 white crochet thread and a size 9 steel crochet hook.

Gauge: 10 sts equal 1 inch
TO SAVE TIME, TAKE TIME TO CHECK GAUGE.

COLLAR
Ch 155.

Row 1: Dc in 4th ch from hook, dc in next 2 ch, 2 dc in next ch, continue across, dc in each ch with 2 dc in every 5th ch, fasten off — 187 dc counting ch-3 as dc.

Row 2: Join thread in 19th dc from end, ch 3, sk 3 dc, tr in next dc, (ch 5, tr in same dc) 5 times, (sk 3 dc, tr in next dc, ch 5, tr in same dc) 35 times, sk 3 dc, tr in next dc, (ch 5, tr in same dc as last tr) 5 times, ch 3, sk 3 dc, sl st in next 3 dc.

Row 3: Ch 3, turn, sc in ch 3 sp, *(ch 5, sc in next ch 5 sp) repeat from * across, ending with ch 5, sc in ch-3 sp, ch 3. Working on Row 1, sk 1 dc, sl st in next 3 dc.

Row 4: Ch 5, turn, working on Row 3, sc in ch-3 sp, (ch 5, sc in next ch-5 sp) repeat from * across, ending with ch 5, sc in ch-3 sp. Working on Row 1, ch 2, sk 1 dc, dc in next dc.

Row 5: Working on preceding row, ch 9, turn, sl st in 5th ch from hook, ch 4, sc in next ch-5 sp, (ch 5, sc in next ch-5 sp, ch 9, sl st in 5th ch from hook, ch 4, sc in next ch-5 sp) 22 times, ch 9, sl st in 5th ch from hook, ch 4, sc in ch-5 sp, ch 2. Working on Row 1, sl st in same dc as ch-3, sl st in 4 dc.

Row 6: Ch 1, turn, working on preceding row, *(4 tr in ch-5 lp, ch 3) twice, 4 tr in same ch-5 lp, ch 1, sc in ch-5 sp, ch 1, repeat from *22 more times, (4 tr in next ch-5 lp, ch 3) twice, 4 tr in same ch-5 lp, ch 1. Working on Row 1, sk 3 dc, sl st in next 4 dc.

Row 7: Ch 5, turn, working on preceding row, sc in ch-3 sp, (ch 7, sc in ch-3 sp, ch 2, tr in sc, ch 3, tr in same sc, ch 2, sc in ch-3 sp) twice, (ch 7, sc in ch-3 sp, ch 5, sc in next ch-3 sp) 19 times, ch 7, sc in ch-3 sp, (ch 2, tr in sc, ch 3, tr in same sc,

ch 2, sc in ch-3 sp, ch 7, sc in ch-3 sp) twice, ch 5. Working on Row 1, sk 2 dc, sl st in 4 dc.

Row 8: Turn, working on preceding row, 9 dc in ch-5 sp, *(13 dc in ch-7 sp, sl st in tr, 5 dc in ch-3 sp, sl st in tr, sk ch-2 sp) twice, (13 dc in ch-7 sp, sc in ch-5 sp) *19 times, repeat between *'s twice, 13 dc in ch-7 sp, 9 dc in ch-5 sp. Working on Row 1, sk 2 dc, sl st in 4 dc. Turn.

Row 9: Working on preceding row, ch 2, sk 2 dc, dc in next dc, ch 4, sk 3 dc, dc in next dc, sk 4 dc, dc in next dc, *(ch 4, sk 3 dc, dc in next dc, ch 3, dc in same dc, ch 4, sk 3 dc, dc in next dc, ch 2, sk 4 dc, dc in next dc, ch 3, dc in same dc, ch 2, sk 4 dc, dc in next dc) twice, (ch 4, sk 3 dc, dc in next dc, ch 3, dc in same dc, ch 4, sk 3 dc, dc in next dc, sk 2 dc, sc and 2 dc, dc in next dc) * 19 times, repeat between *'s twice, ch 4, sk 3 dc, dc in next dc, ch 3, dc in same dc, ch 4, sk 3 dc, dc in next dc, sk 4 dc, dc in next dc, ch 4, sk 3 dc, dc in next dc, ch 2. Working on Row 1, sk 2 dc, sl st in next 2 dc.

Row 10: Sc in each st around except in ch-3 sp, work 1 sc, ch 3, sc in sc just made, (picot), sc in same ch-3 sp, ending by sk 1 dc in Row 1 and sl st in last dc. Fasten off.

TEARDROP COLLAR

ew gifts are cherished more than those hand-made by a close friend or relative. Thrill your loved one this Christmas with this lovely collar, crocheted in an attractive tear drop pattern. You will need two balls of Coats & Clark's "Knit-Cro-Sheen" and a size 10 steel crochet hook.

Starting at neck edge, ch 182.

Row 1: Sc in 2nd chain from hook, sc in each ch across, ch 6, turn.

Row 2: Sk first 3 sc, dc in next sc, *ch 3, sk 2 sc, dc in next sc, repeat from * across — 60 sps, ch 6, turn.

Row 3: Holding back on hook the last lp of each tr, tr in first dc, sk first sp, tr in center ch of next sp, thread over and draw through all lps on hook — joint tr made, *ch 6, make a joint tr by making first tr in same ch as last tr, sk 1 dc, make second tr in next dc, ch 6, make a joint tr, making tr in same place as last tr, sk next sp, tr in center ch of next sp, repeat from * across, making last tr in 3rd ch of ch-6, ch 2, tr in same place as last tr, ch 7, turn.

Row 4: Make a joint tr over first 2 sps, *ch 9, 2 tr in next sp, ch 9, joint tr over next 2 sps, repeat from *, ending with joint tr over last 2 sps, ch 3, tr in 4th ch of ch-6, ch 7, turn.

Row 5: Make a joint tr in center ch of first sp and 3rd ch of next sp, *ch 6, joint tr in 3rd ch and 7th ch of same sp, ch 6, joint tr in 7th ch of same sp and 3rd ch of next sp, repeat from *, ending with ch 3, tr in same place as last tr, ch 4, turn.

Row 6: Tr in 1st sp, *ch 7, 2 tr in next sp, tr in next sp, ch 6, joint tr over same sp and next sp, ch 6, tr in same sp as last tr, 2 tr in next sp, repeat from *, ending with ch 7, tr in next sp, tr in 4th ch of ch-7, ch 9, turn.

Row 7: *3 Tr in center ch of next sp, ch 5, tr in next 2 tr, ch 5, joint tr over next 2 sps, ch 5, sk next tr, tr in next 2 tr, ch 5, repeat from * across, ending with 3 tr in center ch of sp, ch 5, tr in top of ch-4, ch 9, turn.

Row 8: Sk first tr, *2 tr in next tr, tr in next tr, 2 tr in next tr, ch 5, tr in next 2 tr, (ch 4, tr in last tr made) twice, sk joint tr, tr in next 2 tr, ch 5, repeat from * across, end-ing with ch 5, tr in 4th ch of ch-9, ch 9, turn.

Row 9: Sk first tr, *2 tr in next tr, tr in next 3 tr, 2 tr in next tr, ch 9, sk 2 tr, sc between next two tr groups, ch 9, sk 2 tr, repeat from * across, ending with 2 tr in last tr, ch 5, tr in 4th ch of ch-9, ch 9, turn.

Row 10: Sk first tr, *2 tr in next tr, tr in next 5 tr, 2 tr in next tr, ch 6, holding back on hook the last lp of each tr, make 2 tr in 4th ch from hook, thread over and draw through all lps on hook (2-tr cluster made), holding back last lp of each tr, work 3 tr in next lp, thread over and draw through all lps (3-tr cluster made), work a 3-tr cluster in next lp, ch 4, work a 2-tr cluster in 4th ch from hook, ch 2, repeat from * across, ending with 2 tr in last tr, ch 5, tr in 4th ch of ch-9, ch 9, turn.

Row 11: Sk first tr, *joint tr in first and 5th tr of next group, ch 7, sc in 4th ch from hook, ch 3 — picot lp made, joint tr in 5th and 9th tr of same group, make picot lp, 3-tr cluster in center of clusters of previous row, make picot lp, repeat from * across, ending with joint tr over 5th and 9th tr of last group, ch 5, tr in 4th ch of ch-9.

Fasten off. Starch lightly and press.

LACE MEDALLION COLLAR

No matter what the occasion, you'll feel "dressed up" with this lace medallion collar to accent a basic dress, blouse or sweater. The medallion motifs are joined as you work, so the collar is made quickly.

To make this collar, you will need

2 balls (106 yards) of size 5 DMC Pearl Cotton, a size 4 steel crochet hook and 1 pearlized shank button.

Motif 1:

Ch 8, join with sl st to form a ring, ch 1.

Rnd 1: 16 Sc in ring, join. Ch 1.

Rnd 2: Sc in first sc, *ch 5, sk 1 sc, sc in next sc, repeat from * 6 times. Ch 5, join.

Rnd 3: Sl st in first ch-5 sp, ch 4 (counts as first tr), *yo twice, yo and pull up lp, (yo and pull through 2 lps on hook) twice, repeat from * twice, yo and pull through all lps on hook (3-tr cluster made). Ch 5, sc in sc of previous rnd, **ch 5, 4-tr cluster in next ch-5 lp, ch 5, sc in sc of previous rnd, repeat from ** 6 times, ch 5, sl st in top of first sc of previous rnd, ch 5.

Rnd 4: Sc in top of ch-5 before tr cluster, *ch 5, sc in top of ch-5 after tr cluster, ch 5, sc in top of ch-5 before next 4-tr cluster, ch 5, sc in ch-5 after 4-tr cluster, repeat from * 6 times, ch 5, sc in first sc, fasten off.

Motif 2:

Work as for first 3 rnds of Motif 1, ch 5.

Rnd 4: (Joining Rnd) Sc in top of first ch-5 before cluster, ch 5, sc in top of ch-5 after the 4-tr cluster, ch 5, sc in top of ch-5 before next 4-tr cluster, ch 2, work next ch through any ch-5 lp which tops a cluster group on Motif 1, ch 2, sc in ch-5 after 4-tr cluster, *ch 2, work next ch through next ch-5 lp on Motif 1, ch 2, sc in ch-5 after next cluster group, repeat from * once, continue around motif as for Motif 1.

Work 7 more motifs joining in same manner so there is one cluster group with a ch-5 on each side of it free at neck edge. Join with sl st at end of last medallion. Do not fasten off, continue for neck edge.

Finishing: Ch 8 (will be at top of a cluster group), dc in first ch-5 sp, ch 3, sc in next ch-5 sp on top of motif, ch 3, dc in next ch-5 sp, ch 3, tr in joining between motifs, ch 3, dc in first ch-5 sp of next motif, ch 3, sc in ch-5 sp on top of motif. Continue around neck edge, end with sc in top of last motif, ch 3, dc in next ch-5 sp, ch 3, tr in next ch-5 sp, ch 1, do not turn.

Continuing along outside edge, 3 sc in tr just worked, *2 sc in next ch-2 sp, (2 sc, ch 3, 2 sc in next sp) 9 times, 2 sc in next ch-2 sp. Repeat from * 8 more times, end sc in first st at neck edge.

Ch 6 or desired length for button lp. Work 1 hdc in last sc, then 1 hdc in each st around neck edge. Sew button to edge opposite button lp.

CHILD'S PINEAPPLE COLLAR

Your little girl will love this dazzling pineapple-patterned collar.

One collar requires the following amounts and colors of Coats & Clark's "Knit-Cro-Sheen": 1 ball (100 yards) gold and white metallic and 1 ball (100 yards) white. You will also need a size 9 steel crochet hook, a tapestry needle, and one ⅜-inch diameter button to match.

Note: Use #7 steel crochet hook for adult size.

Gauge: 10 ch equal 1 inch

With white, ch 123.

Note: Keep work tight.

Row 1: Dc in 4th ch from hook and in each of next 3 ch, ch 2, *dc in each of next 5 dc, ch 2, repeat from * 21 times, dc in each of next 4 ch, ch 1 for buttonhole, sk 1 ch, dc in last ch. Fasten off, weave in end.

Turn piece (back side of row is right side of collar). Join metallic yarn in first ch-2 sp. Ch 4.

Row 2: *Work shell of (2 dc, ch 2, 2 dc) in next ch-2 sp,ch 1, repeat from * across. Ch 4, turn.

Row 3: *Work shell in ch-2 sp of shell below, ch 2, (dc,ch 3, dc — base) in next shell, ch 2, repeat from * 10 times, ch 2, shell in last shell. Ch 4, turn.

Row 4: Shell in first shell, *ch 2,

INTERMEDIATE

8 dc in ch-3 sp of base, ch 2, shell in next shell, repeat from * 10 times. Ch 4, turn.

Row 5: Shell in first shell, *ch 2, (dc in dc, ch 1) 7 times, dc in dc — Fan, ch 2, shell in next shell, repeat from * 10 times. Ch 4, turn.

Row 6: Shell in first shell, *ch 2, sc in first ch-1 sp of Fan, (ch 3, sc in next ch-1 sp) 6 times, ch 2, shell in next shell, repeat from * 10 times. Ch 4, turn.

Row 7: Shell in first shell, ch 2, *sc in first ch-3 lp, (ch 3, sc in next ch-3 lp) 5 times, ch 2, *(2 dc, ch 2, 2 dc, ch 2, 2 dc — Double shell) in next shell, ch 2 **, repeat from * to ** 9 times and from * to * once more, shell in last shell. Ch 4, turn.

Row 8: Shell in first shell, *ch 2, sc in first ch-3 lp, (ch 3, sc in next ch-3 lp) 4 times, *(ch 2, shell in next ch-2 sp of Double Shell) twice **, repeat from * to ** 9 times and from * to * once more, shell in last shell. Ch 4, turn.

Row 9: Shell in first shell, *ch 2, sc in first ch-3 lp, (ch 3, sc in next ch-3 lp) 3 times, ch 2, shell in next shell*, ch 1, (tr, ch 1, tr — Long V-st made (Lvst), ch 2, Lvst) in next ch-2 sp between shells, ch 1, shell in next shell**, repeat from * to ** 9 times and from * to * once more. Ch 4, turn.

Row 10: Shell in first shell, *ch 2, sc in first ch-3 lp, (ch 3, sc in next ch-3 lp) twice, ch 2, shell in next shell*, ch 1, Lvst in next Lvst, (Lvst, ch 2, Lvst) in next ch-2 sp, Lvst in next Lvst, ch 1, shell in next shell**, repeat from * to ** 9 times and from * to * once more. Ch 4, turn.

Row 11: Shell in first shell, *ch 2, sc in first ch-3 lp, ch 3, sc in next ch-3 lp, ch 2, shell in next shell*, ch 1, (dc, ch 1, dc — V-st in next Lvst) twice, (V-st, ch 2, V-st) in ch-2 sp, (V-st in next Lvst) twice, ch 1, shell in next shell**, repeat from * to ** 9 times and from * to * once more, join white thread; fasten off metallic. Ch 4, turn.

Row 12: *Shell in first shell, ch 2, sc in ch-3 lp, ch 2, 2 dc in next shell, turn work and sc in ch-2 sp of first shell, ch 1, 2 dc in same sp as last dc*, (tr in next V-st, ch 3, sl st in 3rd ch from hook for single picot — spc, tr in same V-st) twice, (tr, ch 4, sl st in 3rd ch from hook, sc in next ch for double picot — dpc, tr) in next V-st, (tr, ch 5, sl st in 3rd ch from hook, sl st in next ch, sc in next ch for triple picot — tpc, tr, ch 7, sl st in 3rd, 4th and 5th ch from hook, sc in next ch, hdc in 7th ch, tr, tpc, tr) in ch-2 sp, (tr, dpc, tr) in next V-st, (tr, spc, tr in next V-st) twice**, repeat from * to ** 9 times and from * to * once more. Fasten off, weave in ends. Sew on button.

WHITE LACE COLLAR

Wear your hair up to show off this charming collar, made with a series of single and double crochet stitches. To make this lace collar, you will need two balls of size 5 DMC Pearl cotton, a size 4 steel crochet hook, and one hook-and-eye fastener.

Note: To increase or decrease collar size, use one size larger or smaller hook.

Row 1: Ch 128 (measures approximately 15 inches), sc in 2nd ch and in each ch across — 127 sc. Ch 3, turn.

Row 2: Dc in each sc across — 127 dc. Ch 2, turn.

Row 3: Yo, pull up lp in first st, yo and through 2 lps on hook, repeat to 3rd st, yo and through all 4 lps on hook (cl-3 made), ch 3, *9 dc, ch 3, cl-5 over next 5 sts, ch 3, repeat from * 8 more times, ending last repeat cl-3. Ch 5, turn.

Row 4: Sc in ch-3 sp, ch 3, *sk 1 dc, dc in each of next 7 dc, ch 4, sc in next ch-3 sp, ch 4, sc in next ch-3 sp, ch 4, repeat from * 8 more times, ending last repeat ch 2, dc in top of turning ch. Ch 5, turn.

Row 5: Sc in first sp, ch 5, sc in next sp, ch 5, *sk 1 dc, dc in each of next 5 dc, (ch 5, sc in next sp) 3 times, ch 5, repeat from * 7 more times, sk 1 dc, dc in each of next 5 dc, ch 5, sc in next sp, ch 3, dc in top of turning ch. Ch 6, turn.

Row 6: Sc in first sp, ch 6, sc in next sp, ch 6, *sk 1 dc, dc in next 3 dc, (ch 6, sc in next sp) 4 times, ch 6, repeat from * 7 more times, sk 1 dc, dc in each of next 3 dc, (ch 6, sc in next sp) twice, ch 3, dc in top of turning ch. Ch 6, turn.

Row 7: Sc in first sp, (ch 6, sc in next sp) twice, ch 4, *sk 1 dc, dc in next dc, ch 4, (sc in next sp, ch 6) 4 times, sc in next sp, ch 4, repeat from * 7 times, sk next dc, dc in next dc, ch 4, sc in next sp, ch 6, sc in next sp, ch 3, dc in top of turning ch. Ch 6, turn.

Row 8: Sc in first sp, *ch 6, sc in next sp, repeat from * across, end with ch 3, dc in top of turning ch. Ch 1, turn.

Row 9: Sc in first ch-3 sp, *(ch 5, tr, ch 5, sl st in first st of ch, tr) in next sp, ch 5, sc in next sp, repeat from * across, end ch 5, sc in top of turning ch.

Finishing: Work 1 row sc up collar front, around neck edge, then down other side of front, fasten off. Sew hook-and-eye fastener to wrong side of ends. Weave in ends and block.

STAR COLLAR

T his dainty flower-and-leaf pattern forms a four-pointed-star collar that will brighten up a dark blouse, dress or sweater. This is a challenging project for the experienced crocheter.

You will need Daisy mercerized crochet cotton size 30 in white or ecru and a size 12 crochet hook.

Flower Pattern:

Row 1: Starting at center, ch 8, dc in starting st, (ch 4, dc) 3 times in same st, ch 4, sl st in 3rd st of beginning ch.

Row 2: Ch 1, (1 sc in next sp, ch 5, sl st in sc for a pc (picot), 3 sc, a pc and 1 sc in rest of same sp, 1 sc in dc) 5 times.

Row 3: Ch 5, tr in same st with last sc, (ch 9, a 2-tr cluster in center sc between next 2 picots) 9 times, ch 4, tr in top of first tr.

Row 4: (4 tr, a 5-ch pc and 4 tr) in same st as tr cluster, sc in next 9-ch lp, *(4 tr, a pc, 4 tr) in lp of next tr cluster, sc in next lp. Repeat from * around. Fasten off.

Leaf Pattern:

Ch 7, dc in first st, ch 8, sl st in 8th ch st from hook, ch 7, dc in 7th ch st from hook, sl st in starting st.

Ch 12, (tr, ch 4, tr) in first 7-ch lp, ch 4, (tr, ch 4, dtr, ch 7, dtr, ch 4, tr) all in end 8-ch lp, ch 4, (tr, ch 4, tr) in next 7-ch lp, ch 12, sc in center sp between lps, *(1 hdc, 3 dc, 1 hdc and 1 sc) 3 times in next 12-ch lp, **(1 hdc, 3 dc, 1 hdc and 1 sc) in each of next 3 sps, (1 hdc, 4 dc, a 5-ch pc, 4 dc, 1 hdc, and 1 sc) all in next 7-ch sp, (1 hdc, 3 dc, 1 hdc and 1 sc) in each of next 3 sps, (1 hdc, 3 dc, 1 hdc and 1 sc) 3 times in next

12-ch lp, sl st in first hdc, **ch 2, sl st in one petal of flower. Fasten off.

†Make another left to *. (1 hdc, 3 dc, 1 hdc and 1 sc) twice in next 12-ch lp, 1 hdc and 2 dc in same sp, ch 4, sl st in center dc of third scallop from end of last leaf, (3 sc, a 5-ch pc and 3 sc) on 4-ch, sl st in last dc, (1 dc, 1 hdc and 1 sc) in rest of same 12-ch lp. Repeat first leaf from ** to **. Ch 2, sl st in next second petal on flower. Fasten off. Repeat from † twice.

Joining Row: With wrong side facing, ch 5, *dc in third st of first scallop below tip end of leaf, (ch 5, sc in the next scallop) 3 times, ch 5, hdc in next scallop, ch 10; sl st in pc on the 2nd petal of flower. Ch 10, hdc in 3rd scallop from stem of leaf, (ch 5, sc in next scallop) 3 times. Ch 5, dc in the next scallop; repeat from * with other 3 sections 3 times.

Edging: Ch 10, turn dc in the 5th ch from hook for button loop and in the next 4 ch. Work 1 scallop (1 hdc, 3dc, 1 hdc) in each 5-ch sp, sc in the next st. In the 10-ch sps work (1 hdc, 3 dc, 1 hdc, 1 sc) twice, end with 5 dc.

FILET COLLAR

Perfect for dressing up a plain sweater or dress neckline, the delicate filet crochet gives this collar a charming lacy look. Try bright or metallic colors for parties and holidays.

To make this collar, you will need one ball (325 yards) of Coats & Clark's Cotton "Knit-Cro-Sheen" and a size 8 steel crochet hook (or size needed to obtain gauge) and a yarn bobbin.

Gauge: 10 dc equal 1 inch
3½ blocks and spaces equal 1 inch
4 rows equal 1 inch
TO SAVE TIME, TAKE TIME TO CHECK GAUGE.

Wind a 3-foot length of yarn on the bobbin.

Ch 75 for front edge of collar.

Row 1: Dc in 4th ch from hook and in each ch across — 73 dc. Ch 3 (counts as first dc of next row), turn.

Row 2: Dc in 2nd dc and in each of next 3 dc, *ch 2, sk 2 dc, dc in next dc (sp made), repeat from * 21 times, 2 dc, dc in top of ch-3. Ch 3, turn.

Work from chart (page 72) through Row 4, ch 20, turn.

Row 5: Dc in 4th ch from hook and in each of next 16 ch, work from chart across row, do not fasten off. Join bobbin yarn in top of Row 4, ch 18, fasten off bobbin yarn. Continue Row 5 across ch, working dc in each ch across — 36 blocks and sps. Ch 3, turn.

Continue working from chart, inc 18 dc each end of Row 9 as in Row 5 — 48 blocks and sps. On Row 25, work left side of collar only through Row 49. Ch 59, fasten off.

For right side of collar, sk 59 dc for neck opening, join thread in 60th dc, ch 3 for first dc and work from chart through Row 49.

Row 50: Work from chart to neck edge, join ch 59 to top of Row 49 (taking care not to twist ch), continue Row 50 across ch and right side of collar (neck opening complete). Work from chart through Row 65. Do not ch at end of row, turn.

Row 66: Sl st across 18 dc. In 19th dc, ch 3, work from chart across row to last 18 dc. Ch 3, turn. Continue working from chart.

Row 70: Repeat Row 66. Work to end of chart. Fasten off.

CHART
FILET COLLAR

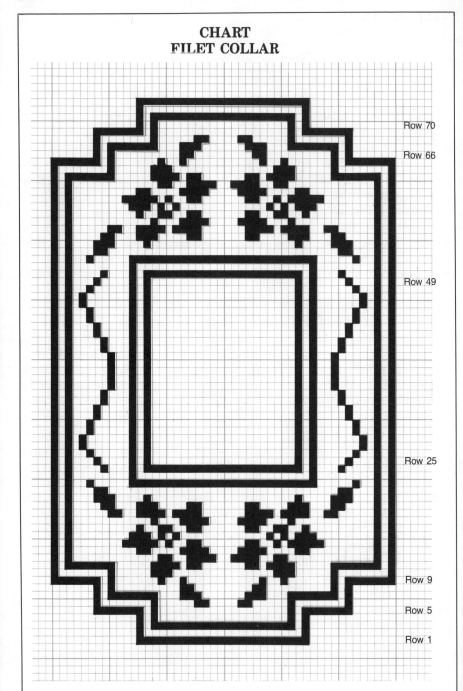

Row 70

Row 66

Row 49

Row 25

Row 9

Row 5

Row 1